THE USBORNE SOCCER SCHOOL

GOALKEEPING

Jonathan Miller

Designed by Neil Francis

Illustrations by Bob Bond * Photographs by Chris Cole

Edited by Felicity Brooks * Managing designer: Stephen Wright

Consultants: John Shiels,

Bobby Charlton International Soccer Schools Ltd.;

Peter Bonetti, Chelsea and England

With thanks to Susan Robinson.
With special thanks to players Osman Afzal, Sajid Aziz, Leanne Davis,
Lindsey Jamieson, Matthew Rea, Ciaran Simpson, Mark Travis, David Wood,
and to their coaches, Dave Benson and Gavin Rhodes.

Library photographs: Action Images and Empics * Cover photograph: Allsport UK
Soccer boots courtesy of Reebok UK

Photographic manipulation by John Russell

CONTENTS

GOALKEEPING BASICS

The goalkeeper is one of the most important players in a soccer team. All winning teams have a very good goalie as well as a strong defense. A goalie's main job is to protect the goal, but he also helps organize the defense, and his kicks and throws can lead to sudden or gradual attacks. This book shows you how to develop the skills and qualities you need to be a good goalie.

WHAT MAKES A GOOD GOALIE?

Decisiveness – you need to be able to think quickly every time there is an attack on your goal (see page 14).

Agility – you will often have to jump, fall and dive as you try to stop a shot at goal (see page 10).

Courage – you will have to dive and jump in crowded penalty areas with many legs, elbows and feet around you (see page 14).

A cool head – if you make a mistake or are faced with a high pressure situation, you need to be able to stay calm and focus on the game (see page 15).

You can find out how to do acrobatic diving saves, like this one, on page 10.

STAR GOALIE

Good coordination – sometimes you will need to change direction very quickly and make fast reflex saves (see page 29).

Good communication – your defense will want to hear clear instructions on 'set piece plays' (see pages 22 and 24).

Positional sense – you will need to be able to vary your position in the goal to make it harder for attackers to shoot (see page 12).

Many soccer experts believe that Danish goalie Peter Schmeichel has played a big part in Manchester United's success.

GOALKEEPING LAWS

There are a number of rules of the game which you will need to know about as a goalie. Soccer laws can change often, so you will need to keep up-to-date with them. Breaking a rule is a 'foul' and a free kick may be given against you.

★ When you have the ball in your hands, you can only take up to four paces before you must release it.

★ After you have taken hold of the ball, you must get it out to your teammates in no more than five or six seconds.

★ You can only handle the ball inside your own penalty area. If you come out of the area, use your feet or head when you touch the ball. Breaking this rule is very serious, and you might get ejected from the field.

★ If a teammate passes the ball back to you, or throws a throw-in directly to you, you cannot use your hands to control the ball. You can handle headers and passes that come off the chest or thigh.

USEFUL KICKING TERMS

This book uses a number of special terms to describe the parts of the foot and the stages in kicking a ball.

*Your **backswing** is when you swing your leg back before you kick the ball.*

*Your **follow-through** is when you swing your leg up after kicking the ball.*

*The **instep** of your foot stretches from your big toe back to your ankle.*

*The top of your foot, but not including your toes, is called your '**laces**'.*

PARTS OF THE FIELD

*The post closest to the ball is called the **near post**. The one farthest away is the **far post**.*

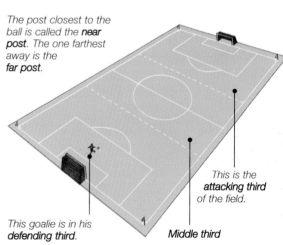

*This is the **attacking third** of the field.*

*This goalie is in his **defending third**.*

Middle third

You will spend most of your time in your team's defending third of the field. When your team is attacking, then play is in your attacking third. The area in-between is called the middle third.

READY TO SAVE

When you think you've got what it takes to be a goalkeeper, then the next step is to get hold of the right equipment and learn the vital goalkeeping skills of quick movement around the goal area and reliable handling of the ball.

GOALIE'S STANCE

When you're waiting to make a save, you should stand in a set position. This allows you to react quickly to attacks on the goal.

Keep your head still and your eyes on the ball.

This is the typical stance used by goalkeepers. It shows you are alert and ready.

Try to lean forward slightly so you are ready to make quick and sudden falls or jumps.

Your hands should be about waist height with palms facing outward.

Your legs should be slightly bent, and about a shoulder width apart.

Your weight should be equally balanced on the balls of your feet.

WHAT TO WEAR

A ball cap keeps the sun out of your eyes when dealing with high balls.

Wear loose, comfortable clothes. Diving and bending isn't easy in tight clothes.

A shirt with padded elbows and shoulders helps to protect you when you dive.

Gloves with latex palms help to give you a much better grip on the ball.

On hard ground, wear sweat pants to help protect your knees.

MOVING AROUND THE GOAL AREA

When you are comfortable with the goalie's stance, you can practice moving quickly around the goal area. If you can move well, catches are much easier to take, as you get more of your body behind the ball. Try moving in the set position, taking small sideways steps. Don't cross your feet as it can slow you down. Ask a teammate to move backward and forward across the penalty area. Try to mirror his movements.

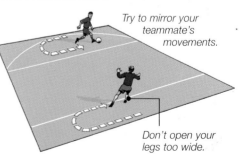

Try to mirror your teammate's movements.

Don't open your legs too wide.

THE W SHAPE

For shots or headers that come toward you at chest or head height, the most effective catching technique is the W shape. The palms of your hands face outward and your index fingers and thumbs form a 'W' around the back of the ball. Your fingers need to be spread wide and thumbs should be about an inch or two (2-5cm) apart.

As the shot approaches, you need to keep your eyes on the ball. If you look away from the ball, this could mean a dropped catch and a rebound to an opponent.

Keep your hands well in front of your body, so you can watch the ball as you catch it.

Make sure your fingers are relaxed and flexible so that they absorb the impact of a shot. The ball might bounce out of rigid, tense hands.

This is how your hands should look when you catch using the W shape.

CATCHING AND MOVING

This game will help you to practice combining your sideways movement in the set position with taking catches at chest or head height.

Lay out a zigzag pattern of sports markers on a field with a gap of about 2m (6ft) between each one. Weave through the markers, staying in the set stance.

After you catch, bring the ball close in to your body, so that it cannot slip out of your hands.

Ask a teammate to throw or kick shots at chest or head height. He should vary the direction of the throws, aiming to your sides as well as straight ahead.

GOOD HANDLING

The W shape is a useful basic catching technique, but because the ball comes at many different heights and angles, you also need to get to know other ways of handling it. No matter where the ball is coming from, good footwork will make handling a lot easier.

CRADLING THE BALL

Scooping the ball into your body is the best method to use with balls that come at waist or stomach height. It is a very safe way of catching, and some goalies use the scoop with chest high balls too.

Cradle the ball with your hands and arms.

As the ball comes into contact with your chest or stomach, wrap your hands and forearms around the back of the ball. Your body will cushion the impact of a shot. Try not to step back as you catch.

As the shot arrives, angle your hands downward, giving the ball a clear path to travel into your body.

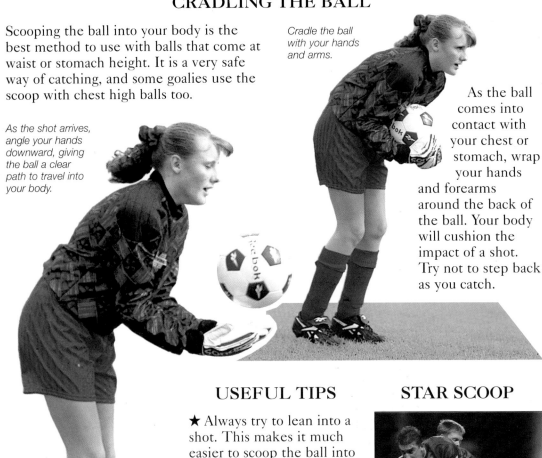

USEFUL TIPS

★ Always try to lean into a shot. This makes it much easier to scoop the ball into your body.

★ You may need to take a small jump to get your upper body behind a slightly higher shot.

★ It's very risky to use the W shape with a waist high shot, as you can't get your eyes behind the flight of the incoming ball.

STAR SCOOP

This Derby County goalie makes a good scoop while under pressure in an English Premier League game.

THE BARRIER POSITION

The barrier is the safer of the two methods you can use for ground level shots. It takes time to get down into this position, so it's best to use the barrier when you have a clear view of the ball or can see the shot early.

Place one knee on the ground, with your leg in the position shown in the picture. Put the foot of your other leg lengthwise alongside it, so that you make a long barrier.

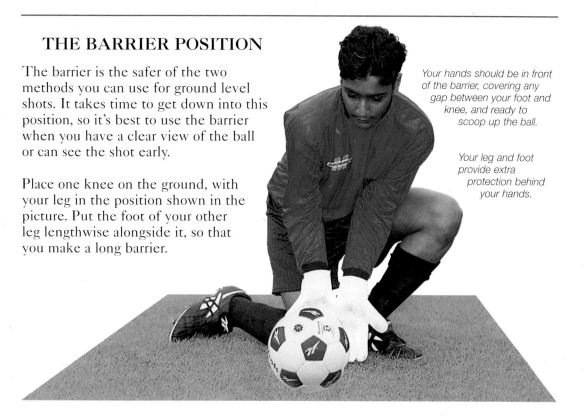

Your hands should be in front of the barrier, covering any gap between your foot and knee, and ready to scoop up the ball.

Your leg and foot provide extra protection behind your hands.

THE BENDING SCOOP

It isn't easy to get into the safer barrier position quickly, so with faster ground shots it's better to use the bending scoop. This position relies upon good footwork and close attention to the movement of the ball.

As the shot approaches, bring your feet close together. Then bend down and scoop the ball into your hands.

It's risky to use this method on uneven playing surfaces and in bad weather conditions. An unexpected deflection of the ball can cause serious problems.

HIGH AND LOW SHOT PRACTICE

This game will help you practice catching shots aimed at different heights. You will need two other players.

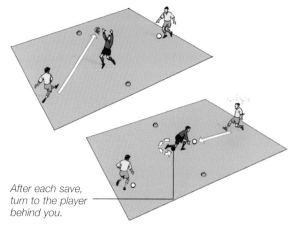

After each save, turn to the player behind you.

Mark out a goal 3m (10ft) wide, and place two teammates 5m (16ft) away on either side of it, each with a ball. One player provides chest and head high shots, the other player hits ground shots. This is a tiring drill, so change around regularly.

SHOTS NEAR THE GOALIE

Some shots come too quickly for you to have time to do a kneeling or bending save. When you need to get down to the ball as fast as possible, falling to the ground is the best solution. Practicing falling saves will help you get ready to try diving saves later on.

THE COLLAPSING SAVE

When a ball is aimed close to you, there is no need to dive for it. What you should do instead is move quickly out of the set stance and collapse onto the shot. When you do a collapsing save, swing your legs to one side and drop down to the ball hands first. Your body will act as a barrier behind your hands. Try not to land on your elbows (see page 10).

Notice how the goalie above is already looking to position his hands behind the ball. Although he has begun to swing his legs to one side, the top half of his body is very steady and focused on the ball.

The goalie puts both hands on the ball. One hand wraps around the back of the ball, while the other is on top.

The wrapping hand acts as a barrier. The hand on top grips the ball to his body.

Once the shot has been stopped, the goalie pulls the ball in close to his chest. He then curls himself around the ball to help protect his body in a crowded goal area.

COLLAPSING TIPS

★ You should practice collapsing saves regularly, because many goalies find them very difficult to do.

★ Don't overdo your collapsing movement. It shouldn't involve any jumping or acrobatic leaps.

★ The ball will be moving fast, so get your hands down in time; otherwise the ball will squeeze under your body.

This goalie didn't move fast enough.

SAVING WITH YOUR FEET

When a shot is fired in from very close range, you will need to react fast to make a save. If you don't have time to get your hands to the ball, you'll have to save with your feet and legs.

As the ball approaches, keep your weight well balanced and turn your feet outward. Watch the ball very closely and try to use your legs as a barrier.

Saving with your feet should only be attempted as a final option. This type of save is instinctive and you have no control over where the ball rebounds.

Saving with your feet is a good reflex reaction when a shot comes at you through a crowd of players (see page 28).

PREPARING FOR DIVING SAVES

Diving saves involve a lot of falling on the ground. Here are two games to give you more practice, before you learn how to dive. It's best to practice with another goalie, who can also get used to falling.

1. Your teammate rolls the ball through your legs. Turn around quickly and fall on the ball before it is out of your reach.

2. Your teammate throws balls 1m (3ft) either side of you. Crouch down to catch them, falling on your side as you catch.

HANDS AND FEET PRACTICE

Mark out a goal about 4m (13ft) wide within the goal area. Place two more markers the same distance apart about 3m (10ft) out from goal. Do the same again about 6m (20ft) out.

Ask a teammate to stand on a line level with either set of markers and take shots at goal. Change with your teammate when you feel tired. Use your hands to save whenever possible.

Practice collapsing saves for longer shots.

Save with your feet and legs for closer, faster shots.

DIVING SAVES

When attackers fire wider shots at goal, you'll need to attempt a diving save. Successful, acrobatic, diving saves give goalkeepers a lot of satisfaction and can make the difference between winning or losing a game. However, there is more to a diving save than simply leaping into the air. The right jumping and landing techniques are essential.

A DIVING CATCH

When you spot the 'flight', or direction, of the ball, take a few quick sideways paces to reduce your diving distance. Stay focused on the ball in the set stance.

Just before you are about to dive, quickly transfer your weight onto the foot nearest to the incoming ball. Push down hard on this foot and then begin to leap up.

Try to get as much 'spring' from your leg as possible. As you leap up, keep your eyes on the ball at all times and dive slightly forward to attack the shot.

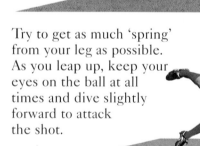

Use the W shape catching technique, letting your hands absorb the power of the shot. Grasp the ball tightly so that it doesn't bounce out of your hands when you land.

A SAFE LANDING

It's very important to learn a safe landing technique. When you hit the ground, try to land on your side, as this is a well cushioned part of the body. Don't come down on your elbows or your stomach.

Keep your body relaxed as you land.

If you are playing on an artificial surface or on hard ground, sweat pants can help prevent painful grazes to the knees.

THE CAT

Many diving saves require impressive agility and suppleness.

In the 1960s and '70s, Peter Bonetti of Chelsea and England became known as 'The Cat', because of his quick reflexes and diving technique.

TIPPING THE BALL

You should try to catch most diving saves, but if a shot is too powerful or too well-placed to catch, you should still try to get a hand on the ball as it goes by.

A slight deflection, or tip, of the ball can be enough to push it off target. When the shot touches your hand, make sure your palm is open and your fingers are spread wide. Try to push or flick the ball away.

Use only one hand to deflect the ball.

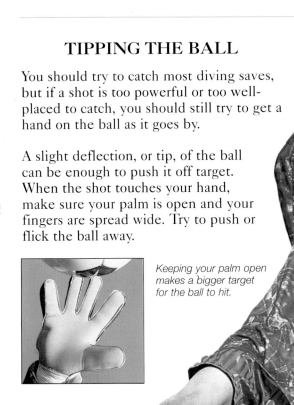

Keeping your palm open makes a bigger target for the ball to hit.

When you deflect the ball away, try to tip it over the bar or around the post.

PLAY SAFE

If you push the ball straight out in front, you could give it to an opposing striker.

The safest option is putting it out of play for a corner. You can tip the ball with either hand as you dive, but try to use the hand nearest to the ball. Use your upper hand for tipping over the bar, and your lower hand for pushing the ball around the post.

DIVING TIPS

★ It is better to use quick footwork to get closer to the ball and make an easier save, than to try a more difficult diving save.

★ All goalies have a favorite diving side but you should be a strong diver on both sides. Spend extra time building up your weaker spring.

IMPROVING YOUR DIVES

This game helps you get used to the hard impact with the ground that follows a diving save. It can also strengthen your spring off the ground. Ask a teammate or another goalie to shoot or throw the ball just inside either post of a full size goal. Stand in the middle of the goal before each shot and as the ball approaches, leap up off the foot nearest to the ball. Trade roles after four or five diving saves.

Try to catch every shot. Only tip the ball away if you have to.

Be careful that you don't collide with the posts. Always watch your position.

POSITIONING

In goalkeeping, good positional sense is as important as sound handling skills, especially when the ball is in the defending third of the field. Good positioning involves skillful footwork and getting your body behind the ball. This makes a lot of saves easier for you and also makes shooting at goal harder for your opponents.

GETTING IN LINE

Goalies like to position themselves somewhere on an imaginary line between the ball and the middle of the goal. This is known as being in line with play.

NARROWING THE ANGLE

Good goalies not only need to be in line, but off their goal line too. By coming off the goal line, goalies reduce the view of the goal for attackers and 'narrow' the shooting angle. Shots become much easier for the goalie to reach.

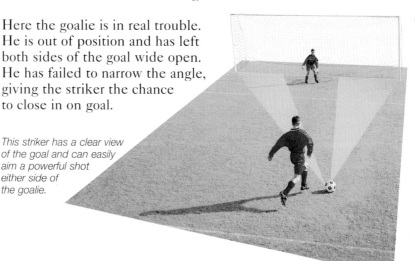

The striker has a small target area.

This goalie is in line with play and so as a shot comes in, he can get his body behind the ball and make a simple save.

Here the goalie is in the perfect position. He is in line with play and has come off his goal line to narrow the angle. He can handle shots to his left or right.

Here the goalie is in real trouble. He is out of position and has left both sides of the goal wide open. He has failed to narrow the angle, giving the striker the chance to close in on goal.

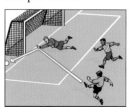

Here the goalie hasn't managed to keep in line with play. As a shot approaches, he is at full stretch and has to make a much more difficult save.

This striker has a clear view of the goal and can easily aim a powerful shot either side of the goalie.

IN THE DEFENDING THIRD

You should always be in line when the ball is in your defending third of the field. How far off your goal line you should be depends on where play is taking place, and if you think that your goal area is under threat of attack from a sudden shot or cross.

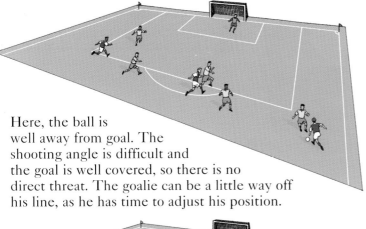

Here, the ball is well away from goal. The shooting angle is difficult and the goal is well covered, so there is no direct threat. The goalie can be a little way off his line, as he has time to adjust his position.

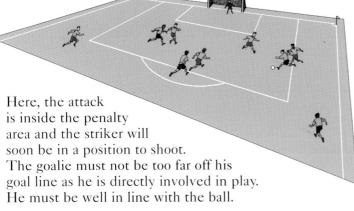

Here, the attack is inside the penalty area and the striker will soon be in a position to shoot. The goalie must not be too far off his goal line as he is directly involved in play. He must be well in line with the ball.

THE CHIP SHOT

A goalie should be well off his line and in touch with play when the opponents are on the attack, but he must not come out too fast.

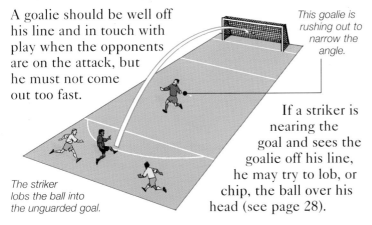

This goalie is rushing out to narrow the angle.

The striker lobs the ball into the unguarded goal.

If a striker is nearing the goal and sees the goalie off his line, he may try to lob, or chip, the ball over his head (see page 28).

RECOVERING POSITION

You must always be ready to change your position quickly. A sudden sideways pass near or inside the penalty area will leave you well out of line. You need to get in line again fast, before an attacker can shoot into the open space.

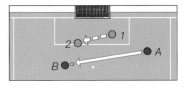

Here, player A passes to player B. The goalie should quickly move from position 1, where he was covering player A, to position 2 to line up against player B. By making a direct diagonal movement, he will get into position sooner.

THE ANGLES GAME

This game helps you practice getting in line with play and narrowing shooting angles. Ask two teammates, each with a ball, to stand on either side of the penalty area about 14m (46ft) out from goal.

Get into line, yell 'ready' and then save from player A.

Do the same with player B. A and B should vary their positions before each shot.

ONE-ON-ONES

A defensive mistake or a great pass can lead to a striker being through on goal, with only the goalie to beat. These 'one-on-one' situations are a real test of technique and temperament for any goalie.

FORCING THE ATTACKER WIDE

You need to position yourself well and react quickly and positively if you are to have any chance of stopping an attacker's run on goal. Don't commit yourself too early to running out, but try to narrow the shooting angle and force the attacker wide, away from goal. This will make it more difficult for him to shoot and will give defenders a chance to get back and support you. Be ready for a sudden shot.

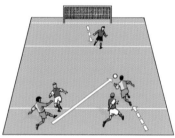

1. As the striker is running onto a pass but has not yet touched the ball, get quickly off your line and narrow the shooting angle.

2. Once the striker has the ball, slow down, and watch out for a shot. Get into the set stance and block the path to goal.

3. As the striker tries to take the ball around you, stay in line and force him wide. It is now much harder for him to score.

DIVING AT AN ATTACKER'S FEET

When a striker attempts to dribble the ball around you, try to gain possession by diving at the player's feet.

This type of save is difficult and you need a lot of courage and a cool head. Only dive if you feel sure you will win possession. Be positive and attack the ball.

The best time to make your move is when the ball is slightly ahead of the attacker and not totally under control.

Go in hands first for the ball. By keeping them in front of your face, you help to protect your head.

SPREADING YOURSELF

As you go down to save at an attacker's feet, try to 'spread yourself' on the ground, making a long barrier between the ball and the goal. This will help narrow the angle too.

Get down low, trying not to leave any gaps between your body and the ground. Once you have claimed the ball, wrap your body around it for extra security.

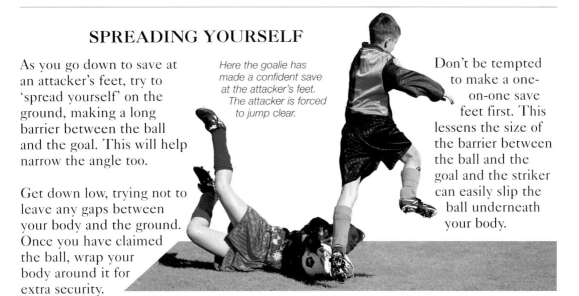

Here the goalie has made a confident save at the attacker's feet. The attacker is forced to jump clear.

Don't be tempted to make a one-on-one save feet first. This lessens the size of the barrier between the ball and the goal and the striker can easily slip the ball underneath your body.

SPREADING PRACTICE

This drill helps you to judge the moment when to dive at an attacker's feet. Mark out a field about 10m (33ft) square. Ask two team-mates to keep possession of the ball as you move around in the set stance, diving at their feet. Don't be tempted to save feet first.

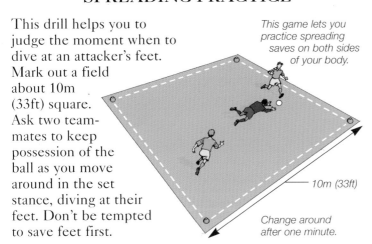

This game lets you practice spreading saves on both sides of your body.

— 10m (33ft)

Change around after one minute.

STAYING COOL

One-on-ones are very pressurized situations. You should try to stay calm and not make any rash decisions. Remember that the striker is under more pressure than you are. He is expected to score and has to decide very quickly how to get the ball past you, and into the net.

If you know your opponent has one weaker shooting foot, force him to take the ball on that side.

Looking big and confident can unsettle a striker – so don't crouch down too far in your stance. Waving your hands or arms around quickly can also affect a striker's concentration.

STAR BLOCK

Here Coventry City goalie Steve Ogrizovic shows a lot of courage and prevents an almost certain goal, by making an impressive spreading save.

He bravely dives at the feet of Newcastle United's Georgian international midfielder Temur Ketsbaia and wins possession of the ball.

HANDLING CROSSES

Many goals come from high crosses aimed deep into the penalty area. Every cross is different, and you need to decide whether to come out for a cross or leave it for your defense to clear. Catch a cross if you can, but punch or tip if you have to. If you decide to deal with a cross, be positive and go for the ball.

POSITIONING FOR CROSSES

Where you stand for a cross depends on where the crosser is. Half turn your body toward the crosser so that you can watch movements in the area as well as the ball.

Here, the ball is near the wing and a long way out from goal. The goalie is well positioned in the center of the goal so that he won't be left stranded by a cross over his head. Moving backward and catching a ball under pressure isn't easy.

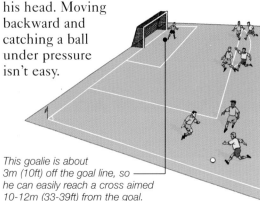

This goalie is about 3m (10ft) off the goal line, so he can easily reach a cross aimed 10-12m (33-39ft) from the goal.

Play has now moved away from the wing and well into the attacking third of the field. The goalie is moving closer to the near post to narrow the angle. He must still be alert to the chance of a far post cross.

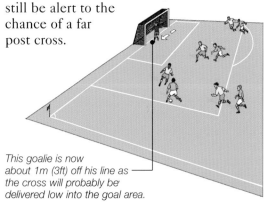

This goalie is now about 1m (3ft) off his line as the cross will probably be delivered low into the goal area.

A CLEAN CATCH

You need good communication with your defense (see page 22) when dealing with a cross. If you decide you can reach an incoming cross and can make a clean catch without other players getting in your way, then clearly yell 'Goalie's ball!' as you take a running jump for it.

Jump off one leg and catch the ball about 30cm (1ft) in front of your face, using the W shape.

Lift up the leg nearest to the opposing side to protect your lower body against challenges.

As you jump, turn sideways to the opposing side and face the ball. Try to catch a cross when the ball is at its highest point. This makes it harder for strikers to get up and reach the ball. When you have caught a cross, be ready to make a quick throw (see page 18) to start an attack.

TWO-HANDED PUNCHES

Sometimes other players can get in your way or put you under so much pressure that you are unable to catch the ball. In this case, try to punch it away instead. A good punched clearance needs height and distance to give you enough time to recover your position if the ball goes straight to an opposing player.

This is how you clench your fists for a two-handed punch.

Aim for the lower half of the ball.

Take a running jump at the ball and yell 'Goalie's ball!' To get maximum power in your punches you need to use two clenched fists. This also offers a larger surface area for the ball to hit. Keep your fists together and strike the ball firmly with the part of your hands between the knuckles and the finger joints.

ONE-HANDED PUNCHES

If you can't get two hands to the ball, you may have to use a less powerful one-handed punch.

One-handed punches are difficult to do because you have a very small punching surface to use.

When the ball is drifting over your head, and you have to move backward quickly, a one-handed punch will strike the ball out of danger toward the opposite wing.

TIPPING

If a cross is aimed deep into the goal area and you are under a lot of pressure, you could try tipping the ball over the bar for a corner kick (see page 11).

Use the hand which is farthest from the goal, to get a much bigger swing at the ball.

When you tip the ball out for a corner kick, you are giving possession back to your opponents. A catch or punch is safer.

CROSSES GAME

This game should get you used to handling under pressure and timing your jumps. Stand in the middle of a goal and ask two teammates, each with a ball, to kick crosses from the wings.

Ask your teammates to vary the height and pace of the crosses.

This teammate acts as an opposing striker, trying to beat you to the ball. Teammates could trade roles regularly.

THROWING

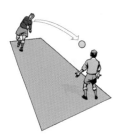

Accurate and reliable distribution of the ball to your teammates is an essential skill for a goalie. Well placed throws or kicks can lead to dangerous attacks on your opponents' goal. There are three main types of throws and each can be effective in opening up space for an unmarked teammate.

THE UNDERARM ROLL

For an underarm throw, start by swinging your throwing arm back.

You use the underarm roll when you are aiming for a teammate no more than 8m (26ft) away. As he will be positioned near the goal, use this throw when no opponents are close by. Don't use this type of throw on muddy fields, as the ball might get stuck.

Get down quite low. Your front foot should point in the direction of the throw.

Swing your throwing arm forward, releasing the ball at the last moment.

Keep the ball low, rolling it along the ground.

THE JAVELIN THROW

Use the javelin throw to cover distances of up to 15m (49ft). Your target might be a teammate who has moved into space on the wing or who has dropped back from midfield. Javelin throws should be delivered low and fast to their target, so try not to throw the ball too high in the air.

Bend your knees slightly to help keep the ball low as you release it.

Bend your throwing arm back and bring the ball up level with your shoulder. Aim your non-throwing arm at the target and point your front foot in the same direction.

Swing your throwing arm forward quickly and release the ball. Flicking your wrist will help keep the ball low. For extra distance on your throw, follow through powerfully.

THE OVERARM THROW

Use the overarm throw to cover distances of 15m (49ft) or more. When your technique is well developed, the overarm throw can travel nearly as far as a kick. This throw is very good for getting the ball upfield quickly once your opponents' attack has broken down. A fast, well placed throw can leave opponents badly out of position and can turn defense into attack.

Bring your throwing arm back behind your body. Keep it straight. Point your non-throwing arm and your front foot at the target.

Swing your throwing arm powerfully upward and over your shoulder.

Transfer your weight onto your front foot. To get height on the throw, release the ball when your arm is at its highest point.

WHEN TO THROW

★ Use a throw after catching a cross. You can change the direction of play while opponents are still in your defending third.

★ If the opposing team has a tall defense, low throws are a lot better than high kicks for keeping possession.

★ When you are playing in a strong wind, use throws rather than kicks – they are easier to direct and control.

★ Stick to throwing if you are not a strong kicker. Good throws are better than weak kicks.

WHERE TO THROW

Most throws should be aimed toward the sides of the field, where a teammate may be able to find some space to run into.

Aim for the safest part of the field.

A throw aimed into the crowded middle of the field will be difficult to control and could be easily intercepted. As most throws travel quite low through the air, you shouldn't try to throw over the heads of opponents.

THROWING GAME

Ask two goalies to help you with this game so you can all practice your throwing skills. Form a triangle, 6m (20ft) apart, and roll the ball underarm to each other first.

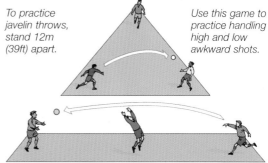

To practice javelin throws, stand 12m (39ft) apart.

Use this game to practice handling high and low awkward shots.

For overarm practice, two throwers stand about 15m (49ft) apart. The other goalie stands in the middle and tries to intercept the throws.

KICKING

Place kicks, volleys and half-volleys give you an opportunity to send the ball a long way upfield, changing defense into attack. Keepers need to be strong, accurate kickers, so practice regularly.

THE PLACE KICK

A place kick is a kick taken when the ball is stationary, such as a goal kick or free kick. Long, powerful place kicks help ease pressure on your defense. If your kicks don't travel very far, make sure they are accurate.

Take an angled run-up and put your non-kicking foot to the side of the ball. Your kicking foot swings forward quickly.

As you kick, lean back slightly and keep your eyes fixed on the ball.

Strike the lower half of the ball with your laces. Follow through powerfully.

THE VOLLEY

To do a volley, you drop the ball from your hands and kick it before it hits the ground. When you are holding the ball, you can take four steps as a run-up before you kick (see page 3). The higher you aim a volley, the longer it will take to reach its target.

As you run, hold the ball waist high in front of you. Take a good backswing as the ball drops.

Place your non-kicking leg behind the ball. Leaning back slightly will help to get lift on the kick.

Keeping your head steady, kick the bottom of the ball with your laces. Follow-through smoothly.

THE HALF-VOLLEY

When you do a half-volley, the ball bounces once before you kick it. Use half-volleys in windy conditions, as they do not travel as high through the air as volleys. It's risky to try them on muddy or uneven fields.

Drop the ball from waist high level. It should land in front of your non-kicking foot.

As the ball bounces, swing your kicking leg forward, leaning back as you kick.

Watching the ball carefully, strike the bottom half of it with your laces.

WHICH KICK TO CHOOSE

Think carefully about what type of kick to use and don't take any chances. Aim all place kicks to the sides of the field, and never kick across the penalty area. Only kick over your opponents' heads with high volleys or half-volleys.

If you are a strong kicker, you might be able to reach the attacking third with a powerful volley.

Half-volleys travel more quickly than volleys and so are good for starting fast, unexpected attacks.

Place kicks aimed to the sides of the field are safer and might find teammates in space.

If your strikers are not good at heading the ball, a short kick to a defender is better than a kick upfield.

TARGET PRACTICE

You will need five or six balls for this game which will improve the accuracy and distance of your kicks. Ask another goalie to help you. Take turns at kicking and retrieving the balls.

For place kicks, kick alternately from either corner of the goal area, aiming inside two markers 6m (20ft) apart on the halfway line.

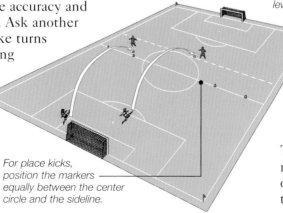

For volleys, position markers level with the circle in the other half of the field.

For place kicks, position the markers equally between the center circle and the sideline.

For half-volleys and volleys, kick from the edge of the penalty area. Try to clear the markers in your opponents' half of the field.

HELPING THE DEFENSE

Although as a goalie you have your own important job to do, you should remember that you are part of the defensive unit. A good goalie will communicate with his teammates and be on-hand to receive back passes and cut out through balls.

TALKING TO YOUR DEFENSE

From the goal area, you have a good view of the field and can see how play is developing. This allows you to advise your defenders about what they should do and warn them about possible dangers. You should yell clear, short instructions. Decide with your teammates before a game what you will yell in different situations. There are several well-known, regular yells.

'Goalie's ball!' – yell this to claim possession in any situation, and especially for crosses (see page 16).

'Peter, pick him up!' – tells a specific teammate to mark an opponent who is unmarked.

'Push up!' – gets your defense to move upfield, possibly catching opponents offsides (see page 23).

'Man on!' – warns a teammate with the ball who is unaware that an opponent is about to tackle him.

'Time!' – tells a teammate with the ball that no opposing players are near enough to challenge him.

'Well played!' – tells a teammate that he has done good work. Always try to encourage teammates.

KEEPING UP WITH PLAY

Try to stay in line with play even when the ball is not in your defending third. If you are always in touch with the game, you might be able to offer some support to your teammates in tricky situations.

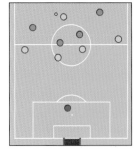

Here play is in the attacking third. The goalie is on the edge of the penalty area, ready to deal with long clearances and through balls.

Play is now in the middle third and the goalie has moved back slightly. He can cut out through balls or long-range shots as well as receive back passes.

PLAYING AS A SWEEPER

A good goalie will be ready to act as another defensive player when needed. Although you will spend most of your time in your penalty area, by moving slightly upfield you can really help your defense.

If a teammate wants to pass the ball back to you, stand a few meters back from him, in case he overhits or misdirects the pass.

Be ready to take on the role of 'sweeper', a spare man at the back of the defense. You can clear up any loose balls and can be on-hand to receive back passes from defenders.

When you receive a back pass, remember that you can only use your hands with headers, not with passes from feet.

THE OFFSIDES RULE

All goalies need to know about the offsides rule. You can often stop dangerous attacks by catching opposing attackers offsides. Your team is then awarded an indirect free kick.

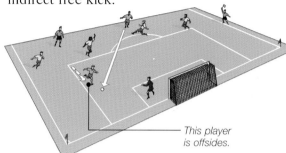

This player is offsides.

A player is offsides when, just as a pass is made to him, there are less than two opponents between him and the goal. No player can be offsides in his own half or if he receives the ball directly from a corner, throw-in or goal kick. Asking your defense to push up to catch strikers offsides is risky. If an attacker gets past a defender who has pushed up, he is through on goal.

CLEARANCE KICKS

You will sometimes be in position to intercept dangerous through balls with a powerful one-touch clearance which aims to force the ball well upfield or out of play.

Accuracy is not so important with these kicks, but you must react quickly and kick powerfully while under pressure. Only come out of your area if you are sure you will get to the ball first.

Try to make good, strong contact with the ball for a powerful clearance kick.

CORNER KICKS & THROW-INS

Corner kicks and throw-ins in your defending third give your opponents the chance to use a 'dead', or stationary, ball to carry out some preplanned moves, called 'set piece plays'. The fact that no player can be offsides if he receives the ball directly from a throw-in or corner kick makes these moves dangerous.

ORGANIZING CORNER DEFENSE

As goalie, you are responsible for making sure that your defenders are in a good position and that no opposing attackers are unmarked. Most players in your team will have a particular job to do on a corner kick, whether marking opponents or covering parts of the penalty area. Yell clear instructions to your teammates and take charge of the situation, making quick, confident decisions.

One or two players should cover the far post and the area in front of it.

One player should guard the area around the near post, with another player nearby to cover a very short corner.

Other players should mark opponents who have come forward for the corner kick.

You should stand in the center of the goal, about 1m (3ft) off your line, so you can deal with a near or far post delivery.

One defender should stand on the edge of the goal area to give the goalie extra support.

No defender can come any nearer than 9m (30ft) to the corner taker.

THE NEAR POST MOVE

One of the most dangerous and commonly used set piece plays at a corner kick is the three-touch move which involves an inswinging corner to the near post.

The aim of this move is to get the ball into the goal using just three touches. An attacker swings the corner in to the near post where a tall opponent tries to flick on a header toward the far post. Another player tries to get in front of his marker to meet the flick-on with a header or shot.

Here, to deal with a near post move, D1 and D2 must stay goal-side of A1.

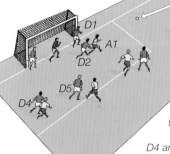

The goalie should be positioned in the center to deal with any flicked-on headers.

D4 and D5 must stay close to their markers.

THE OUTSWINGER

The outswinging corner kick is aimed at players on the edge of the penalty area who will run in and head the ball at goal.

An outswinging cross

To catch an outswinging cross, come out fast as the ball will be moving away from you. It might be better to let defenders deal with it, so be ready to make a save.

THE SHORT CORNER

Short corner kicks allow opponents to keep possession of the ball while they decide whether to cross or try a long-range shot.

A short corner kick

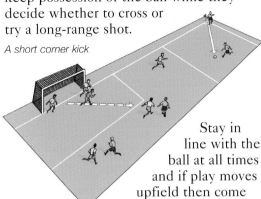

Stay in line with the ball at all times and if play moves upfield then come off your line too. Your defenders should keep marking in case of a sudden cross.

LONG THROW-INS

Long throw-ins are becoming very popular as a way of getting the ball into the goal area. Most teams will have a player who can easily throw the ball deep into the penalty area. Treat long throw-ins like near post corner kicks, as your opponents will try to use a three-touch move.

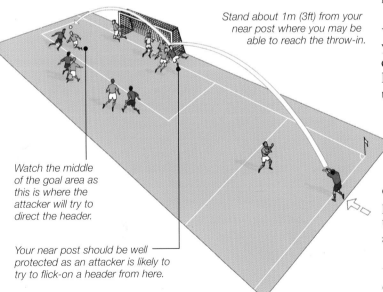

Stand about 1m (3ft) from your near post where you may be able to reach the throw-in.

Watch the middle of the goal area as this is where the attacker will try to direct the header.

Your near post should be well protected as an attacker is likely to try to flick-on a header from here.

SET PIECE TIPS

★ Stand near the middle of the goal at corner kicks, so you can cover any part of your goal area. Watch the kicker and any movements in the penalty area.

★ Don't get blocked on your line by players crowding in front of you. Move around on your line to make some space.

★ You should treat corner kicks the same as crosses (see page 16). If you think you can safely deal with the ball, then be positive and go for it. Try to take charge of your goal area and be decisive.

★ Short throw-ins in your defending third can be dangerous. Defenders should mark the attackers in and around the penalty area and you should be ready for a cross.

You should be able to tell when a long throw-in is about to happen. The thrower will take a long run-up before throwing and your opponents will push taller players into your penalty area.

FREE KICKS AND PENALTIES

Penalty kicks and direct free kicks, where the taker of the kick can shoot straight for goal, give your opponents a good scoring opportunity. You can organize defensive cover on free kicks, but penalties are a challenge for you alone. They give you the chance to pull off a great save.

CENTRAL FREE KICKS

To reduce the chances of a goal from a central direct free kick, you need to form a defensive wall. You and your teammates should work out in practice where everyone is positioned for free kicks and who will organize the wall.

In a game, if you are organizing the wall, you need to do it quickly before your opponents catch you out of position. The wall must be at least 9m (30ft) away from the kick. It should be lined up slightly past the near post to make swerve shots more difficult.

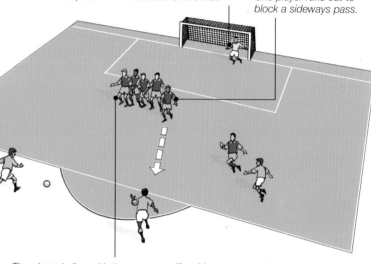

The wall covers the near post, and the goalie covers the far post.

To see the kicker clearly, the goalie stands well to the side of the wall.

There should be about five players in a wall. One player runs out to block a sideways pass.

The player in line with the near post must be fairly tall to make chip shots harder.

If a chip or swerve shot gets past the wall, you may have time to move across and save it.

WIDE FREE KICKS

There is less chance of a shot from a wide free kick, so the wall does not need so many players in it. A two or three player wall can block a deep cross into the goal area. Stand in the center of your goal about 2m (6ft) off your line.

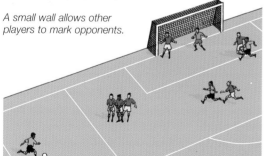

A small wall allows other players to mark opponents.

KICKS INSIDE THE AREA

Indirect free kicks, where the ball has to touch another player before it enters the goal, can be awarded in the penalty area. These can occur in very dangerous positions, so bring as many players behind the ball as possible.

For central kicks, the goalie should rush out as the kick is taken.

SAVING PENALTY KICKS

The outcome of a penalty kick can decide the result of a game, but all the pressure is on the penalty-taker, because his whole team will expect him to score. Before the kick is taken, you can move from side to side if you want to. You can't move forward until after the ball has been kicked.

Moving from side to side along your goal line may help distract the penalty-taker before he takes the kick.

Watch to see if the taker keeps looking at one particular side of the goal before he kicks. But don't assume he's definitely going to shoot in that direction – he may be trying to trick you. Try to delay your dive until the kick has actually been taken. Don't try to anticipate a shot – react to one.

Use any technique to save a penalty. Fall slightly forward as you dive to put more power behind a tip and keep the ball out of the goal.

FAKING TACTIC

A fake is a clever way of fooling your opponents by pretending to move in one direction but then actually going in the other. You can use a fake to try to make a penalty-taker shoot at the side of the goal you are going to dive.

1. As the taker runs up to kick, fake left or right, as if you are about to dive to this side.

2. Dive to the opposite side. The taker may be fooled into shooting where you want him to.

WATCH THE RUN-UP

Watching the penalty-taker's run-up may tell you which side of the goal he is aiming for. Straight run-ups are difficult to predict, because the kicker may choose either side or may kick straight ahead.

Angled run-up – left-footed shot goes to the left.

Curved run-up – right-footed shot goes to the left.

Angled run-ups can result in shots aimed at the same side of the goal as the kicking foot.

Curved run-ups often lead to shots into the opposite side of the goal to the kicking foot.

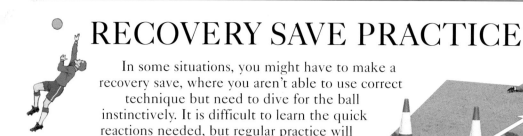

RECOVERY SAVE PRACTICE

In some situations, you might have to make a recovery save, where you aren't able to use correct technique but need to dive for the ball instinctively. It is difficult to learn the quick reactions needed, but regular practice will help sharpen up your reflexes.

DEFLECTED SHOTS

If a shot is fired low into a crowded penalty area, there is a chance that it may bounce off a leg or foot, and change direction. You could then be left well out of position.

To practice saving deflected shots, put a row of three heavy 1m (3ft) high markers 6m (20ft) out from goal, with a gap of 60cm (2ft) between each one. Ask a teammate to stand 5m (16ft) farther back and fire shots at goal. Some shots will deflect off the markers.

You have to react very fast to save a deflected shot. If you are wrong-footed by a deflection, try to save with your feet (see page 9).

Only move after the shot has been made.

Keep your weight well balanced and don't dive too early.

OVERHEAD LOBS

If you are caught out of position, an attacker may lob, or chip, the ball over you. As lob shots travel slowly, you have the chance to recover your position with quick footwork and make a save.

To practice this, place a marker 6m (20ft) from the center of the goal and ask a teammate to stand on the penalty spot with a ball. Run out and touch the marker.

As you touch it, your teammate throws the ball over your head. Step back quickly and leap up. Try to tip the ball over the bar (see page 11).

This game should improve your jumping technique.

As you step back, turn sideways slightly so that you face the ball more.

THE REFLEX SAVE

When there are many players in front of you, blocking your view of play, you might have to react very quickly to deal with a shot that you only see at the last moment. To practice reflex saves, stand in the center of the goal with your back to a teammate who stands about 12m (39ft) out from goal.

You will need to react fast and make a reflex, or instinctive, save.

When your teammate yells 'Turn!' he shoots at goal while you turn around and try to make a save.

Your teammate shouldn't aim too far away from your body and should vary his position before each shot.

Don't worry about your technique. Catch a shot if you can, but if not, try to block or tip it. When you see a low shot very late, saving with your feet might be the best option (see page 9). Practice regularly to speed up your reflexes.

THE FOLLOW-UP SAVE

Whenever you make a save but do not keep possession of the ball, always get back into position quickly, so that you are able to deal with a follow-up shot.

This game will help you practice getting in line with the ball, making a save and then rapidly recovering your position.

This game is very tiring, so rest after each pair of saves or trade with another goalie.

Stand in the center of the goal and ask four teammates, each with a ball, to position themselves an equal distance apart, 15m (49ft) out from goal. Get in line and save from the player farthest to the right. Then save from the next player along who shoots just as you complete the first save. Repeat the exercise with the players on the left.

Your coach could number each striker from 1 to 4 and then yell out one of the numbers. You then save from this player.

PREGAME PREPARATION

It's important that you develop a regular routine before a game, so that you are well prepared, both physically and mentally. You should approach a game with a positive attitude, feeling fit and confident. Just before a game, make sure you do warm-ups and some handling practice.

PREGAME TIPS

★ Try to get a good night's sleep before a game and don't do anything too energetic the day before. It's best to be well rested and alert.

★ Be careful about what you eat before a game. You need to eat well to give yourself energy, but don't eat a large meal just before exercising.

★ Spend time getting your clothing ready. Take items, such as sweat pants and a ball cap, which will be useful in different types of weather.

★ When you arrive at the field, check the quality of the playing surface and keep an eye on the weather conditions, as these might affect the game.

★ Try not to get too nervous in the build-up to a game. Getting worried and stressed wastes a lot of energy, so stay calm and relaxed.

★ Before you warm up, discuss defensive tactics with your teammates, to make sure everyone knows what to do at set piece plays and corner kicks.

STRETCHING AND LOOSENING EXERCISES

Warming up before a game is essential. If you don't loosen up your muscles, you could get injured. Exercise for about ten minutes until you feel warmer, but don't tire yourself out. After finishing these exercises, do some gentle jogging.

To loosen your neck muscles, gently roll your head around in a circle ten times. Then do the same the other way around. This is a very relaxing exercise.

To exercise your shoulders and arms, bend well forward with your legs 30cm (1ft) apart. With your hands on your shoulders, roll both arms around.

To loosen your hamstring muscles, lift up one leg and bend the knee back until you can hold your ankle in your hand. Then do the same with your other leg.

BALL WORK

Getting the feel of the ball will help your handling during a game. Basic routines will improve your timing and get you focused.

Some of the exercises earlier in the book such as high and low shot practice (see page 7) would be ideal, as are the ones below.

Move the ball in a circle around your body, passing it from one hand to the other behind your back. Start waist high and slowly move up to chest level.

Lie on your stomach with your arms in front of you. Ask a teammate to throw catches to you from about 2m (6ft) away. Raise your legs as you catch.

To sharpen your reflexes, ask a teammate to stand 2m (6ft) away holding a ball chest high. When he drops the ball, try and catch it before it hits the ground.

STAY FOCUSED

During a game you may not touch the ball for long periods, but stay focused at all times, or you may start making mistakes. Always use good technique and never get casual about making saves.

This goalie stopped concentrating for a moment and is now unable to get to this long-range shot.

BE CONFIDENT

As the last line of defense for your team, you need to seem confident at all times.

American goalie Kasey Keller shows his confidence by claiming a catch early on in a game.

If you appear nervous, the opposing team might think your technique is weak and could try to pressure you. Believe in your own ability to play well and remember that you are a crucial player on your team.

INDEX